God has brought me through: so many things. The pain behind the life of Octavia D.

By: Octavia D. Hardaway

This book is dedicated to my late Grandma Sarah Amos, my Grandfather Jesse Phifer. My uncle Oswie Lee Amos. To my late Pastor Dr. Ruby L Veal I love you thank you for teaching me how to live a saved life. My cousin Charlie, and Mr. Gary Chambers thank you guys for inspiring me to press forward. These two men believed in my dreams when I didn't believe in them myself. I would also like to remember my first cousin Terrance who passed away in 2012. A lot of your qualities are inside of me.

Thank You's

First given honor to God my Father who is the head of my life, and without him I would be nothing. Thank you father for all the many talents you have blessed me to have. I thank you for the gift of the Holy Ghost, and I thank you for the calling you have given me. I thank you for my visions and dreams! Special shout out to my church family- New Spirit Revival Center! My Pastors: Dr. Darrell, and Belinda, and Pastor James and Michelle Davis.

My family shout outs!

My Madre- I thank you for everything you have done for me and my brothers. I thank you for not aborting me, and I thank you for supporting every dream I have. No matter what accomplishment I achieved you could have been sick or whatever no   matter when I looked in the crowd you was right there cheering me on! Thank you for introducing me to Christ at a young age, and thanks for allowing me to grow up in the church. Thanks for allowing me to be your best friend, and your daughter! Thanks for allowing me to grow into the woman I am today! I owe you everything Mama! What would I do without you? Grandma Phifer- I love you! You are amazing. I pray that I live as long as you and be wise just like you! You inspire me.

My God Mom Min Lynn Greathouse! Thank you for being you! You are so positive and you keep me uplifted! Your words of encouragement mean so much to me! Thanks for adopting me as a daughter. To Evangelist Dunbar! I love you! Thanks for all the talks as I grew into this Proverbs 31 woman I have become! Mama Anita Davis-

Thanks for all the encouragement you have given me throughout the years! God bless you.

My father- You not always being present in my life was an empty space in my heart. My brother's unconditional love towards me filled that space. I love you, and I pray one day we establish a relationship and make up for lost time one day.

My big brother (My Bobby) - Your presence in my life has been a pleasure. I love you so much! You have always been so positive and have always supported every dream I have had. You believed in me when I didn't even believe in myself. I can hear you now "Pooh you can do it". Thanks for treating me like a little princess when I was growing up, and still to this day! Thanks for loving me! Thanks for being my big brother!

My sister in law Toya- I love you so much! You are my role model! We are like best friends I can tell you anything. You have always been there for your bratty little sister. Words can't express the gratitude that I have and glad I was blessed to be your sister.

 My big/ little brother Missle- I love you! Your presence in my life is important. You're very meek, humble, and quiet. Although you rarely say anything I know that you are proud of me! I enjoy being your sister. I'm going to make you guys so proud of me!

Special Great Aunts: Leana and Elizabeth thanks to you both for being a positive reinforcement in my life! Reminding me constantly how proud you guys are of me! Thank you! To all my Aunts and Uncles maternal and paternal I love you all.

To my entire family on maternal and paternal family I can't shout you guys out one by one its way too many. Just know that I love you all, may not see you, or call you, but love for you is in my heart.

My adopted siblings Roger, Rontora, Anthony (TNorm), Stevie, Toy White and Shana I thank God for you all. I love you all and thank God every day for blessing me with siblings like you all. I love you all to pieces!

My nieces and nephews: De'Forest, Daze, Dabriel, Da'Liyah, Milliona, Devon, Da'Jani and special cousin Mariah. I love you guys and everything that I do I do it for you. You guys inspire me even when I feel like giving up the thought of you guys make me strive harder.

Lakeisha, Ashley, Cordell, Tatiyanna. I missed out on a great deal of you guys life, but Auntie loves you all too!

Special Mentors/ Adults In my life- My favorite most influential teachers- Miss Longville, and Mrs. Alyse Reeves- Clark. Mrs. Poole, you and Mr. C have always supported me in my academics. You guys took a liking into me you two saw "my light" and I appreciate everything you have ever done for me. Ms. Bridget- Thanks for being awesome and encouraging me as I enter my new field. I greatly appreciate you being a well down to earth person! Thank you! Sis. Sheila Oldaker you have been so awesome! I thank God for placing you in my life! You are very inspiring! Your words of encouragement shall dwell with me forever. Mrs. Williams, Patricia White, Cassandra Hammond, and everyone that didn't give up on me! I would like to say thank you!

Special thanks to: Sis Eleanor and Sis Elaina, The late Sis Carol Waters, Sis Kenyatta and family. Sis Minni, and Sis Sykes, Sis Shelia. Since the age of 16 I have had the best mentor who is always willing to help in any way possible Mrs. Sheila Smith thank you for all you do! Sis Dana, Sis Dana Cherry, Sis Kendra, Sis Kelly, and Sis Brandee you guys have always been there giving me so much support throughout my adolescent through my adult hood thank you all so much. I appreciate the encouragement so much when I'm broken.

Sis Toni Williams thank you for always giving me encouragement words! You encouragement me when I'm down and broken and make me see myself in a different way. Sis Z you are so sweet you empower me and encourage me as if I'm your little sister! Sis Denise- I call you the woman of power! Thanks for all the prayers you are so anointed by God!

Special friends- My best friends Kiaren, Katy Cronin, Christina, Crystole Ford, Eureka, Courtney Ponder, Branden Burrows, Cedric Lewis, Saundra, Sis Melissa, James, Akelah, Nisha, Naomi, Takia, La'Tisha, Kapri, Lorie Blake, Elisha, Rudy, Ashley, Kevin Gay, Vanessah, Karen Jeffers, Indya, Joycelyn, Angelica (thanks for all the encouragement).Keisha, Shaketa, Lateka, Tedra, Chagrin, Chenay, Kim, Toy. Mama Marianne, and Mama Mary, Nia, Jasmine, Myka, and Dominique, shout out to all of Buchtel High School Class of 2004! Love ya'll.

To my future husband I pray for you daily! Every day when I wake up I thank God for you even though I don't know where or who you are! The thought of knowing that God created you just for me means so much to me! I love you future husband of mine, and I'm patiently waiting on your arrival.

Chapter 1: **Overcoming the fear of death**.

My mom was in the kitchen cooking breakfast when I told her "Mom I'm going to write a book". My mom quietly sat down the dish rag and came out the kitchen, and said what are you going to write about Dear? I told her I'm going to write about my life. I want to encourage somebody that may be going through. My mom went back in the kitchen with a grin and said "Well you're a testimony"! I sat there all day dwelling on my childhood, and spent hours looking through old journals.

I remember telling my sister Rontora who is an author herself I'm going to write a book! She said do it and don't let nobody stop you. "Your life is a testimony somebody needs to hear about it". This inspired me more. The fact that my testimony could help someone made me thrilled to get my story out.

I started reflecting back on my childhood. Growing up during testimony service they would frequently sing a song "If God has done something good for you stand up on your feet". I can truly say that God has done so many great things for me! I was raised

Apostolic/Pentecostal in a strict house hold. My mom did the best she could raising three kids on her own. My father left us when I was just 1 years old. My mom had many worries how was she going to provide for her 16, 4, and 1 year old kids, but the Lord made a way he always does!

My mom was very down and out and didn't know who or where to turn to. She often found comfort in watching Pat Robinson on the 700 club, and one day everything he said was directed towards my mom that day. I can remember her telling me that "it was like he was saying everything that I was going through". I enjoyed growing up for Mama to tell us stories about how she grew up.

So after that incident my mom called our cousin Balina and asked her about church. My mom started going to church with Balina to an Apostolic church name Refuge Tabernacle of the Apostolic Faith Church in 1989. My mom didn't know it yet but this was the turning point in her life that she had been waiting for finding God. My mom was baptized in the name of Jesus and received the gift of the Holy Ghost June 7th 1989. Mama raised us up in the church and made sure we attended church on a regular basis. I really enjoyed church even as a little girl. I can remember my mom would go to Lenten's and buy me all different types of tambourines. I taught myself how to play. I would be at home in the mirror singing a song and playing the tambourine. On weekends me and my brother would dress up and play church. The church was instilled in us even as small children. I loved my pastor so much Pastor Veal.

Pastor Veal was what I would call an angel on earth. That was one amazing woman! Pastor Veal was always there for me whenever I needed her to be. I was always a happy little kid, polite, shy, quiet, and well behaved. I didn't give my mom any trouble. I always excelled high in school. I was a child that enjoyed school I didn't cry when my mom took me to Kindergarten I was excited.

Third grade was a rough year for me. One of my male classmates stuck me in my arm with a pencil. I can remember telling my big brother on the way home from school one day, and he said I'll have to beat him up he probably made you have lead poisoning. I didn't quite understand what that was at the time. I gulped real hard, and anticipated on getting home to my mom because she would know the answer. As soon as I got in after Mom asked us about our day, and we ate our snack and got settled for our homework I would ask her. "Mama what is lead poisoning"? My mom told me that it came from chipped paint and that it could make you really sick if you don't get treated.

I slowly looked at my arm, and I said could someone die from it? My mom looked at me and said yes honey its possible. I frantically went upstairs in my room to hold up my sleeve to look at the tiny mark. Could I have lead poisoning? Could this make me die? I'm an eight year old third grader. I remember weeping slightly for a while, and then I went to pray. I'm glad that I have a praying Mom she taught us to pray as small children. I prayed and asked God to please not let me die.

"Niecy", my mom called me downstairs, yes Mom what are you doing Scooby is bringing Anthony over. Yes I was very excited to see my baby nephew. I was very honored to be an Auntie and I thought I was the coolest kid ever. I played with my nephew for a while and then I started worrying about my arm again. My mom and I have always been best friends I can tell her anything! I remember praying "Dear God please don't let me die amen", but this time my mom heard me. My mom furiously asked me why was I weeping and why did I say what I said? I told her what had happened at school, and she said she would be at the school Monday morning.

She called Bobby, and he talked to me and I felt a little better for that moment. I didn't think anything else of it until Sunday after church when I realized that I had to go to school the next morning. My mom kept her promise she talked to my teacher about what happened and my classmate received a detention for his behavior. I was very quiet at school that day and wasn't very talkative. I waited after school on the playground for my brother, so we can meet Mama and walk home from school.

Mama thought that the problem had been solved, but the problem escalated worse. The next day at school my classmate said give me that pencil four eyes or I'd stick you again. I'm not getting stuck with that pencil again. I remember asking Ms. L can I move to a different seat, and she let me. This time on the walk home I didn't even mention it. I had made up in my mind I was done with school at eight years old. The next morning I remember getting ready for school and I was almost late. I was too busy washing my hands for about 20 minutes. I remember my brother asking my mom why is she washing her hands so much?

I had started falling apart. Finally I was all ready for school. I was fine the whole walk but as soon as I seen Schumacher's Playground I would panic. I started screaming I made my brother scared he didn't know what was wrong with me. Missle pushed me into the building and I started screaming to the top of my lungs I want to go home, I don't want to be at a lead poisoned school. Everyone was confused I loved school, why did it all of a sudden change? I want to go home now; I don't ever want to come back here again. I remember Mr. P the guidance counselor calling my mom.

I remember as if it was yesterday. "Mrs. Hardaway, this is Mr. P calling from Schumacher I have Octavia here she is really upset, would you like to talk to her"? By the time I got on the phone with my mom I was wimping from crying so hard. I remember my mom said "Sweetie Mama is older I can't keep walking back and forth to get you from school what's the problem"? I just want to come home Mama. So my mom came to pick my brother and I up. I knew she would Mama was one of the only few people I knew I could always count on.

One day started turning into weeks. So finally my mother decided enough is enough she talked to Pastor Veal about it. Pastor Veal and I had a great relationship growing up. So finally one day my mom and Pastor Veal came and signed me out of school. I was so happy. I would feel like a new kid outside of Schumacher Academy. Pastor Veal took me to the library, and she spent a whole day with me. I remember her praying for me, and after that day I didn't have those attacks again. It was just something about when she prayed God would always answer speedily. So that was nipped in the bud no more thoughts of death, no more compulsiveness, and no more attacks that regards lead poisoning.

2nd Timothy 1:7 For God has not given us the spirit of fear; but of power, and of love, and a sound mind.

Chapter 2: **Overcoming wanting to be a follower.**

The other day I had a conversation with one of my friends, and she asked me what made me want to live a saved life? I started reflecting back on my childhood, and got emotional but I gave her a lengthy reply. I have always loved God and acknowledged him as my savior, but it wasn't until I received the Holy Ghost for me to receive a complete understanding. I was about five years old when I said that I was going to be different and stand out. The bible tells us that we are a peculiar people, and that we should stand out in the crowd.

Growing up in the church was amazing I would always sing, and participate in church. I told my friend that was not enough my life was still empty. At eleven years old I yielded and accepted God's call and was baptized in the name of Jesus, and spoke in tongues as the spirit of God gave utterance. After July 13th 1997 my life was finally complete! I felt so much happier. I thank God for saving me, I felt amazed that he called me. Matthew 22:14 says it best "For many our called but few are chosen".

In middle school I was the different one. I remember kids constantly picking on me. Some of my nicknames were: Skinny Minnie, skirt girl, and bible girl, preacher girl. I won't lie some of the hurtful scars I have ever carried came from the mouths of my peers.

Even though they may have called me names I never changed. Mama always taught us that if you deny Christ he will deny you. I never played with God because I fear him that's how I was taught. I was the laughing stock among my peers growing up. I would be the only one in study hall instead of the school dances, parties and etc. I never tried to go I obeyed the rules that I was taught to embrace as an adolescent.

Kids would always question me hey why do you wear skirts all the time? I would proudly say because it's my religion that's why! I would never try to pretend like I was something more than what I was. It's sad some of the kids that I wanted to be friends with in school turned out to not be so successful in life. I went on telling my friend I find no fault in Jesus Christ he is alright with me. Growing up a lot of people teased me because I was different. I would always read the scripture that God would make my enemies my footstool. That is so true some of my worse enemies growing up have turned out to be my best friends.

I'm forever bringing up to them remember when you didn't like me. Their reply is how could I have never liked such a woman of faith as you? We often laugh and reminisce about the past. I thank God for the Holy Ghost it has really brought me through a lot of hard times I had to encounter. I would never sacrifice the person I was to fit in any crowd. I always show the real Octavia Denise you can like it or love it.

I would speak proudly of my religion, proudly talk about how I was going to be a virgin until my wedding night, and proudly speak of how I was going to be a Wife and not a Baby Mama. I was determined to finish high school and go off to College and graduate with a Criminal Justice Degree. I had my whole life planned out! I decided and made a commitment to God when I was eight years old that I would present my body to him as a living sacrifice and I'm serious about it.

I recently started a Mentoring program for young women at my church, and I'm teaching them the importance of living holy. I'm teaching them that it's nothing wrong with standing up for Christ. You can be saved and still have fun! I'm a living witness. As a 27 year virgin I can honestly tell you that I'm glad that I was a leader and not a follower.

I sometimes sit back and reflect on how would my life have turned out if I would have followed the crowd? If I had given into temptation, and lived a life of corrupt and sin. It brings tears to my eyes and I'm so glad that I'm a Virgin, that I have never stepped foot in a club, that I have never put an alcoholic beverage to my mouth, or a cigarette, or that I don't use foul language, party, or do the evil corruption of this world.

I'm glad that I decided to live a Holy life. The same people that were always questioning my every move wanted me to fail. I'm so glad that I had a mind to do the right thing, and now I'm a living testimony to others. People have called me "Holier than thou, and said I stick my nose down people who live what we consider ungodly.

I have learned that people that say things like that feel guilty about the actions they have decided to make. How could I ever stick my nose down on someone when I go out of my way to help others?

I'm so glad that I'm not a follower, and I'm also glad that I have learned how to not receive negative things into my life. As Christians we have authority to receive and not to receive what people speak in our lives. If I would have allowed negative influencers in my life I wouldn't be an example today. I have been blessed and honored to be able to have the ability to draw people to Christ. It's amazing because just today one of my coworkers was going through something and they said you need to have Octavia pray for you.

I was so overwhelmed with joy that they think so much of me that they come to me for prayer. It makes me feel so good, and I always tell people it's all God. I take none of the credit I'm doing it all for his glory!

I have been a light to so many people in this dark world. I often think to myself if I would have followed the crowd where would I be? How could I have drawn to Christ? How would my life be now? I'm thankful I had a choice and I chose to live for God! Now a day's people are all about claiming sets and hoods. I'm so glad I serve Jesus and I know in whom to place all my trust. I told my friend if I was to rep and claim anything it would be pertaining to Jesus. I would say I always represent Jesus, and the heaven is the set I claim!

1 Corinthians 11:1 '" Be ye followers of me, even as I am of Christ" (KJV).

Chapter 3: **Overcoming Disappointment**

I have always been the black sheep among family members outside of my immediate family, church, and school. When can I ever catch a break? I would often ask myself. A family is supposed to be of love, but it's filled with hate. A church family is supposed to build you up but yet I felt torn down. I could expect the kids at school to be negative and tear me down. I expected better treatment from my family and church members.

Like I mentioned before I was raised in the church but I went to a church where I didn't fit in, and they made fun of me a lot. My self-esteem was lowered I went through many years of agony but God brought me through it. I was in the third semester of my sophomore year of high school when my Mom's health took a spin. If you truly know me then you know I'm a Momma's girl. I ended up missing over 45 days of school that year. It all started in December my mom would eat certain foods and be in pain, and it would go away.

I'll never forget the day after Easter 2002 my mom was ill and this time nothing seemed to ease the pain. I would beg Momma plenty of days to go to the hospital to see what was wrong. I would cry I hated to see her in so much pain. My mom replied if I go to the hospital where would you go? I said mom don't worry about that I'm fifteen years old. I sometimes blame myself and I sometimes blame my father.

Had I been an adult my mother may have not ended up with half of her colon removed. If my father would have been a real father and a husband and stayed with his family he could have taken care of me while she was hospitalized. Bobby had a big responsibility he had to take care of his own children, and my mom, my brother, and I were also his added on responsibilities. He always came through and made sure that every bill was paid, clothes were on our backs, and that we had food in our stomachs.

I'll never forget the month of April 2002 when my mom had to be hospitalized for seventeen days. Those were the hardest and longest seventeen days of my life. My mom taught us to walk in faith so I always tried to. I was hurt, angry, and confused constantly thinking who to blame for this.

I remember the day when my mom had surgery as if it was yesterday, and seeing the afraid look on her face. She talked to each of us separately before they wheeled her back to the surgery room. I was first her baby, her only birth daughter, her best friend, and she told me not to worry and kissed my forehead. Missle is the meek and quiet one you never know what he is feeling he rarely speak on things. She spoke softly to him, and then lastly her first born.

It was a very emotional time for all of us. I remember sitting in those hard chairs with my siblings, my nephews, a few family members, and a few people from church waiting, and waiting. I remember some people saying I hope she make it through. Now I won't lie I did cry, but I knew God's ability. I did say to myself Lord please don't let anything happen to my mom. Where would I go? What would I do? I can remember going down to the chapel to pray. I began to pour out my heart to God, and offered him my petition on my mother's behalf.

I expressed to God that he knows that our family has never been close, and my father had on and off again been in my life. All I had to depend on in this world was my Mommy, and my oldest brother and sister in law. My brother had a life of his own it wouldn't be fair to him to have to take me in. Bobby was 29 years old at the time, and God knew I needed my mom. I was blessed that my sister Toya took me in while my mommy was in the hospital. Toya made sure I had a meal, that I did my homework, and that I went to see my mom every day. I commend her so much she didn't let my brother leaving her stop her for caring for our family. Besides God nothing in this world can compare to moms and family.

Mothers are so sacred and I cherish my mom daily for that reason alone. I did have Bobby, Toya, and Missle to rely on, but that was pretty much it. I knew that I could go over my great Aunt Leana's house, but she is older and I didn't won't to be an inconvenient. On my Dad side of the family the closest cousin I had was deceased. I knew that if Cousin Charlie was alive he would have helped out. Cousin Charlie helped my mom out with us while we were growing up. At this point in my life I had a lot of emotions to deal with and with little support. I had somewhat support from the older saints at the church but none of the youth was there to support me. I couldn't understand my mom the woman who taught us how to love, and she showed love to everyone at the church, but why wasn't love shown to me and my brothers in our time of need?

I am so thankful to say What a Mighty God we serve God brought my mom through! I was so thankful that God spared her life. Although I had to grow up a young age, and learn how to take care of my family. I didn't mind. I even made up all the course work that I missed those days I was out of school, and yes I was promoted to a Junior that next year. God is so faithful.

I was so worried about how I was going to complete all that homework, do errands for my mom, clean the house, and take care of my mom during her recovery. God gave me the extra strength that I needed to get through. I would tell anyone that's faced with adversity to keep pushing through, and never complain and watch God bring you through.

I didn't have any support from any of the young people from my church. Yet I always had to give out get well cards, birthday gifts if their parents invited me to a party even if I didn't attend the event. What have I ever done to grow up and attend the same church with the same people and for them to dislike me? Was it jealously, Envy, or Ignorance? I was very hurt and went through a stage of with drawl.

My life had changed but I was thankful that it could have been worse, but still it had changed. Growing up me and my mom would catch a bus and go to the mall shop, eat, and hang out. I miss those days just thought about some of those times today. Since my mom's surgery she can't get out as much as she could when I was growing up. I never hold it against her it's not her fault. At times when I'm at the mall by myself I see daughters with their moms, and I can feel warm tears streaming down my face.

At times I find myself watching moms interact with their daughters and have a sudden smile reflecting on the close relationship me and my mom established as a small child. My mom has overcome a serious ordeal and I thank God for sparing her. Mom has become a homebody she just likes to stay in the comfort of our own home. I'm shy but I'm kind of a people person.

Disappointment had entered my life and it made me change. I wasn't the same sweet, quiet, soft spoken girl. I was always angry at someone. I didn't get over this pain until I was ready to admit that I was hurting. I would constantly tell myself I don't care how people treat me it doesn't hurt my feelings. I had gotten used to the feeling of rejection. I had constantly been rejected by family, church family, classmates. The only person that never rejected me not even once was God.

I can remember a lot of people telling me I'm going to be a testimony to some young lady one day. I would often ask myself why would I want to help somebody get through pain? No one beside God was willing to help me. Throughout my life I have had many visions and dreams! I have learned that you can't walk into your true destiny until you accept the calling God has for you! I knew that the gift of ministry and empowerment was over my life, and it had been confirmed many times.

At 25 years old I accepted and embraced this call. I founded my own ministry RHEA (Reaching, Helping, Everyone, Always). I love empowering individuals. I had to overcome the feeling of disappointment in order to get to my destiny. Being disappointed almost stopped me from learning my calling helping others. I'm glad to be able to allow my struggles to help someone else go through theirs.

If someone is reading this book that has went through disappointment, I just want to encourage you to ask God to purge your heart and take it out. Remember that God has never left you nor forsake you. Remember that greater is he that is within you. If God bring you to it he will bring you through it. Don't allow disappointment to stop you from reaching God's plans for your life.

Ending scripture in regards to Disappointment- Colossians 3:23-25

"Whatever you do, work heartily, as for the Lord and not men, knowing that from the Lord you will receive your inheritance as your reward. You are serving the Lord Christ. For the wrongdoer will be paid back for the wrong he has done, and there is no partiality.

Chapter 4: **The battle with low self-esteem and self-image.**

Growing up I was constantly picked on for being skinny and dark skinned. Growing up I was tall, dark, and slim, with long legs, long silky hair, and glasses. I would hate looking in the mirror I didn't like what I saw in the mirror. I remember one time after having a talk with Pastor Veal she asked, "Octavia, why don't you like looking in the mirror? I told her because I don't like what I see looking back at me.

She sat in her chair quiet for a moment rubbing her finger across her lips, and pulled out a tiny yellow tablet. I thought she was going to have me write affirmations or some scriptures on it. She started drawing, and I was amazed I never knew she could draw. After she completed her drawing she wrote on it, and handed it to me. Pastor Veal asked me to look at the drawing she said do you like the picture, and I said yes, and she said well good because that's you.

I was amazed at her work now I had looked in the mirror every day and didn't see that pretty girl I saw on the paper. I couldn't wait to show my mom the picture. I folded it up and put it in my purse and showed my mom after we got home from church. I'm sitting here talking to my mom reflecting on my self-esteem issues and we are laughing and reminiscing on how God has brought me through. I went through a time where I tried to get my breast to grow larger. I remember in eight grade guys told me to eat a lot of cornbread, and grits if I wanted to become thick. I would eat pans of cornbread hoping to gain weight.

My main problem with my self-esteem and self-image was allowing guys opinions of me to change how I saw myself. When I was real skinny guys complained and said I was too skinny, and when I gained weight I was too chunky. I spent so much of my time trying to please others and to do whatever to make them happy.

I would allow the evilness of guys to get into my heart and make me question myself. I was often told that dark skinned girls are often guys last pick, and they didn't like that I wore long skirts, and that my face was makeup less, or that I didn't wear tight clothing. Guys have told me that you had to look at me several times to see my beauty because I'm so covered up.

I often grew frustrated with myself. I can remember when I was about 24 saying that I was going to change my appearance. I was willing because of these low life guys to go against what I stood for and change to make them happy. I can remember that same day when I was planning on getting clothes that I would never wear a scripture kept playing in my mind. "Man look at the outward but God looks at the heart".

That meant so much and it spoke to my situation. God knows that I like dressing conservative and that's how I was comfortable dressing. I didn't have to please these guys. I thought to myself if I change myself I'm changing the work of God. God made me I'm his image. Thinking I'm ugly is like saying God's work is ugly. It's such a huge contradict.

So I've learned to accept myself for who I am Octavia D. I can remember in high school it was a popular song by India Arie "Video". That was the story of my life. Guys would constantly say they want women that look like the women from a BET Video. I wasn't willing to compromise myself to dress prerogative and to disrespect myself for a man that hasn't given his life for me.

Mama always taught me "To leave something to a man's imagination". Everything mama taught me has stuck with me more so much now since I'm an adult. I'm a woman of virtue why should I dress like a Jezebel to get attention? The bible says who can find a woman of virtue for her worth is beyond rubies (Proverbs 31:10).

I won't sit here and lie to you and say that I have the best self-esteem, but I can tell you God has brought me and my self-esteem issues along way. I have been tormented by some of the remarks that guys tell me, but all I can hear is "One man's loss is another man gain". I know that God will bring the man that's deserving of this Proverbs 31 woman in my life when he is ready.

The Holy Ghost has taught me how to accept myself for who I am. I tell guys up front what it is and its either they accept it or leave. To the young women that are battling with self- esteem I dare you to put your trust in God and not man. I started researching and I learned that there are 54 scriptures in the bible that deal with self-esteem alone. I started speaking God's word over myself. I started praying and asking God for healing of words that should have never been spoken to me, all the relationship hurt I had to let it all go. This is how I have been getting through my esteem problem praying and fasting. I encourage my own self, and believe what I say.

Proverbs 31:30 "Charm is deceitful, and beauty is vain, but a woman that fears the Lord shall be praised".

Chapter 5: **Overcoming bruises from the church, and family hurt.**

Church hurt is one of the hardest pains to ever get over at least it was for me. It took a very long time for me to be free from the pain that I was caused from the church in which I grew up. At 19 years old I branched out on my own and went off to another Apostolic church and I was hurt there as well.

I never stopped going to church, but I did stop going to church in a sense. I would be at church every Sunday and would be scared to join the choir, the praise team, the usher board, or etc. All I could think about in my head was why should I go through this again? Why should I even try? So I wouldn't I would just go to church and praise God and go home. I wouldn't talk to nobody; I had a hard time trusted people after my experience from Refuge. After years and years of being tormented by some of the young people I became numb, and I had adopted that feeling and thought it was okay to be treated as such.

I would miss out on a lot of events because I was afraid to be around certain church members. Who would want to be around somebody who hurt them, and caused nothing but strife in their life? I would always find myself trying to ignore people from the past when I came into contact with them.

I will say this growing up I was proud of my church, and proud of my Pastors! I love everyone from that church. I can now say at 27 years old I have released all the pain and mistreatment I have experienced from Refuge at the altar. I can proudly say that when I come into contact with the ones responsible for my pain I can say Praise the Lord. I can hug them, and tell them I love them.

Sitting in church crying tears of sorrow for getting mistreated, and emotionally abused for years played a part on my self-esteem problems. The healing process can't fully begin until you at first forgive all the people involved in the situation. A few years ago I remember getting down on my knees after reflecting on the pain I experienced, and prayed and called out each individual name by name. I felt the heaviness and the hurt come up from my stomach. I was finally free after carrying around that hurt for the past 22 years of my life! God can free you it may take years but I declare he may not come when you want him, but he is always on time. I just want to encourage someone who may be carrying around past pain from church members give it to God. I declare when you give it to him, and allow him to heal you things will fall into place.

Romans 12:19 "Beloved, never avenge yourselves, but leave it to the wrath of God, for it is written, Vengeance is mine, I will repay, says the Lord".

Growing up my Mom and my siblings and nieces and nephews were my world. Growing up without Grandparents was tough for my siblings and I. I would find myself always wondering and day dreaming to myself thinking about what would they be like? I have never seen a picture of my Grandma Sarah Mae Amos. I was fortunate that Bobby had a chance to meet her, and he tells me stories about her. What I have learned is that my Grandma was a very strong woman, and she raised a strong daughter my mom. My mom also raised a strong daughter!

Just the other day I was on the phone with my brother for two hours laughing as he tells me stories about my Grandma. Growing up we kind of knew not to ask Momma questions about her because it would make her emotional. My Grandma was just 49 years old when she died, and my mom took on the responsibility of raising her two younger brothers. My mom didn't have help from family members raising them either. I think that's why my mom and I are so close we both know what it feels like to be rejected by your own family. My mom often considers herself the black sheep of the family as well.

Even though I would have given anything growing up to have had the chance to meet my Grandma my life was empty without her. Grandparent's day was empty, and not having someone to call Nana was odd. It was strange not having a grandmother in my life to help us. Even though we didn't have her, I thank God that whatever we lacked growing up and that my mom couldn't provide my Bobby did. I really didn't have any outside relationships with family except for my own immediate family my brothers, nieces, and nephews, and mom.

I started reflecting back to when I was growing up and my mom was battling with depression and she was scared to stay at home with us we went over our cousin house. Even though I was six years old I didn't like the fact that a family member was taking advantage of my mom. My mom would have to give her half of her check for us to stay there, and my mom bought food but she charged her to cook for me and my brother. Our cousin charged to wash my hair, wash our clothes, let's put it like this she charged for everything she did for us. I was confused my mom and her are first cousins, how could she do this to my mom?

I remember one time she left my mom and I while my mom was at the doctor. I was just six I didn't have a phone to call someone for help. God strengthened my mom and she was able to call Pastor Veal, and she picked us up. My brother and I hated to go back to this house. Growing up having to face her was a challenge! I would get angry every time I thought about that. So you can see my family is very unstable and that's why I tend to stay to myself.

I would be jealous of my friends who would constantly say my Auntie bought me that. I would say hmm must be nice. My friends would say yeah what do you get from yours? I would say nothing and they wouldn't believe me. I'm back to questioning how could my mom constantly give to people and she never received anything in return? I still couldn't understand this for a long time. I would really get frustrated by this. My family has never been close and it's a big family filled with a lot of jealousy, and envy. I can remember plenty of negative comments that were made by family members as I climbed the ladder to my success.

My brother would always say never let your haters make you, but work overtime to break them. That motto stuck with me. I would work harder to make sure that I accomplished everything some would say that I couldn't achieve. I can remember plenty of times when my own family would say negative things about me. I can remember remarks being said that would hurt my feelings. Hearing what my brother taught me constantly played in my mind and I fought hard to prove them wrong.

Everything they thought or said I wouldn't do I accomplished it. I remember they would say I would not learn how to drive a car but I did. If God is for me who can be against me?

I can say no matter what my mom has always supported me and she made sure she attended every ceremony I had. My mom never was one to brag on my academics, and for that reason she rarely told me she was proud of me. I could tell by her facial expression when people would speak on my behalf that she was proud.

I used to pray and ask myself what was wrong with me? Why did certain family members pick on me? Why did certain family members treat me like dirt? I can say now at 27 years old it doesn't matter. I'm living to please God. I have my mom, church family, siblings, nieces and nephews and my few friends they are all I need. I've experienced a lot of hurt and torment from my own family members.

I used to hold it against them, but when you are truly saved and love Jesus you will let it go. I mean cousins used to torment me in school, and turn people against me for no reason at all. I used to be cautious around those cousins and used to try to stay away from them. I can truly say that I have let that go, and I'm free, and not nervous to be around them. God has brought me through that it was very hard to go through, but he brought me out! The guys I had dated in the past would always ask why I don't be around my family, and I would hate to tell them why. Now when a guy ask me that I just say well I'm at a different place in my life God has brought me through some stuff, and I won't ever pick it back up.

Carrying around family hurt for years caused me to be bitter and jealous of other friends that had loving family members. I never experienced that it's okay I've let it all go! I feel so much better since I let that pain go.

" Put on then, as God's chosen ones, holy, and beloved, compassionate hearts, kindness, humility, meekness, and patience, bearing with one another and, if one has a complaint against another, forgiving each other; as also the Lord has forgiven you, so you also must forgive". Colossians 2:12-13

Chapter 6: **Being delivered from bad friendships/ Relationships.**

It's late at night and my mom is sleep and I'm still up typing and reflecting. As I sit here and type tears rush down my face. I'm so thankful God has truly brought me through so many things! I can't include everything he has brought me through in this book for it would take years to create.

Now I'm relaxing thinking about some of the worst friendships/relationships I have had. Mom always taught us that people come into your life for a season, and be careful because everyone that enter your life don't always have great intentions. If you truly know me then you know that I truly love people and I love helping people.

I started seeing who my real friends were when my mom got sick, but I was still a teenager I didn't know what I know now. I had friends that would use me whenever they needed me I was always there for them, but when I needed them they were nowhere to be found. People would always say that one day I would open my eyes and learn who is for me and who is against me. Well I have definitely learned who is real and who wasn't in my life as far as friends. I can remember graduation day from college when friends claimed they were going to be at my celebration, and didn't show up, or I would call them for a favor and no response.

I declare when you find your back up against the wall you shall see who your real friends are. I had plenty people in my life that I needed to get rid of, but couldn't find the courage to separate myself from them. I can remember plenty of times praying and asking God to remove people that I don't need in my life, and he did! Having friendships that aren't on the same level as you is a detrimental to your growth. I can remember mama always telling me "You are either going to pull them, or they are going to pull you. Many of these friendships needed to end long ago, but I didn't have the courage. God said ask and it shall be given unto you. In my adult life I have grown so much in God, and I'm proud of myself. I'm so glad that I have gotten over the hurt of establishing friendships with people that didn't deserve my friendship.

It's time to get deep into my life, I want to show the readers the true pains behind my life relationship hurt. Over the years I battled with low self-esteem. It all started with my childhood through high school crush Brandon. I wasn't blessed to have my father in my life, but I was blessed beyond measure to have my brother. I was shown at a young age how to be treated like a real lady. I was treated like a princess growing up everything I ever wanted my brother would get it for me.

My mom would often tell him to stop spoiling me because he was going to make me rotten, and I chuckle because she was right. My brother would always teach me how to allow a guy to treat me, and he even taught me how to defend myself in case one would ever decide to get violent on me. (Sigh) as I think about those talks on the Frederick block on weekends when I spent a night over my brother and sister in law house.

I met Brandon in sixth grade when I met him I had no interest in him. At this time I was just eleven and my focus was on my academics. He spent many years trying to get my attention. I was very mature and responsible my mom had decided for me to date at age sixteen, but because she trusted me I was allowed to date at fifteen. Of course all my dates had to be chaperoned, and my big cousin Moniqua would always come with me.

At first Brandon was so sweet, always giving me compliments but it suddenly changed after years of dating and seeing that I wasn't going to lose my virginity. You want to talk about having your esteem crushed or lowered I truly know the feeling. I can remember him calling me stupid, dumb, and I can remember him saying "yeah you're even lucky I talked to you you're a two". I was crushed. I couldn't believe how this guy spent years of trying to get my attention could make me feel like nothing. I was so confused I never thought I would end up dating him. He was so interested in me when we were younger why the sudden change?

Now that I'm older I often think and reflect on that it has stuck with me over the past years. I often question my looks now. But I can say God truly does make his people the head and not the tail. B has apologized for his careless behavior, and has admitted that I was a good catch for him. I have learned that people who try to belittle you are having issues within their self and looking for somebody to bully to make their own self feel good.

I can remember one day watching a preacher on the word channel, and he said when you pray for a mate be specific in what you want. I never thought you could be specific like that to God. I hurriedly went into the closet and prayed to God. I remember telling God I want a virgin man, a man that loves him, a man that loves his mom, and a man that's going to be nice to me. He had to have the two J's (Jesus and a job). I started working at a discount store my senior year of high school and I suddenly found the man that had some of the characteristics I had been praying for. Keith and I started dating my freshman year of college.

He was a virgin, he loved God, he worked, he treated his mom right, and he was nice to me, there was only one problem he was non-denominational. I was always taught that if you want a successful relationship/marriage you had to be equally yoked. I didn't quite understand why at that time I was just about to turn nineteen. I can remember many nights explaining to my mom but he is still a virgin mom. I would often try to have tarrying service with Keith over the phone I was desperate to try and help him complete his salvation. I was desperate to help him speak in tongues and receive the gift of the Holy Ghost.

I was Keith's first girlfriend and because of past hurt from B I hurt him a lot. I wasn't ready for marriage and I wasn't ready for a committed relationship like he was. I didn't know then what I know now. I allowed him to talk down to me when he was angry, and I didn't think anything of it. I would often cry but I guess being talked to any kind of way was something I had gotten used to.

I know that I wasn't raised to allow men to treat me disrespectful. My mom taught me at a young age of how a man should treat me. I appreciate that my mom never took my Dad back because he mistreated her. I didn't have to worry about things like other girls I know. There was no boyfriend coming in the house for my mom, and it sure wouldn't be one spending the night.

So where did I pick up this trait of allowing guys to disrespect me? I would often blame myself for the way he treated me. Later in life I learned that it wasn't me that he was controlling. Keith would tell me how long and when I would have to spend time with him I couldn't breathe. This was a stressful relationship and time of my life he would often try to get me to miss out on my classes just to be around him. I wasn't used to this.

I liked to have my own space, and my education was very important to me. I knew that it was time for a change when he started giving me ultimatums between him and my education. Why should I choose a person that belittles me when he is upset with me? Keith would always throw things up to my face when he was mad things I had told him about my past relationship. He would say mean things to me and I would allow it.

He would often say my mom don't like you, or she think I can do better. The saying "Never judge a book by its cover" is real. This lady didn't know me she didn't know my story so why was she judging me? There are always two sides to a story. God delivered me from that relationship. I'd admit it was hard at first but prayer made it a lot easier. I knew my worth, I accepted it, and I embraced it. He would always try to hang with me after he had ended an unsuccessful relationship. Sometimes as a dummy I would accept invitations to hang out with him. Not for long God granted me strength, and I would stop answering his calls, I wouldn't reply to his texts, or his face book messages!

Why should I continue to go back to garbage? God has delivered me from the scars that he placed on my life, so why should I pick it up again? I took a step of faith and moved on with my life knowing and believing God had better for me.

Who would have known that three years later I would meet another negative man? I had just started working at a discount clothing store, and I was in my Junior/Senior year of college. I was twenty three years old and ready for marriage. I had been seeking the Lord and asking him to prepare me for marriage. It's funny that in the beginning guys always know exactly what to say. This one was thrilled and excited to meet a pure woman, and claimed that he had been celibate for years.

He entered the relationship on a bad note asking could he go out on a date with an ex-girlfriend. I thought it was kind of odd, but I kept my cool. I had no idea that something as small as that would escalate to bigger things. One day on the phone with him he told me "You know I had to look at you several times before I could see your beauty you are always so covered up". Of course I took it as a criticism. I went on to ask him what do you mean? He said I'm used to dating woman that are petite and look like a girl from a BET video.

I was so hurt I immediately ended the conversation. Here this 34 year old man is acting like a 23 year old guy. He was older I expected better from him. I felt disrespected in the worse way. I had just got my self-esteem right to where it needed to be. Here this adversary is coming in trying to knock me off of my grind. I snappily told him that I can't help the way I was built and that God created me just the way he intended for me to be.

I thought that it would get better but the negativity got worse. Lanier had started tearing down my self-esteem as if it was his nine to five job. It was something that he got a kick out of. I would talk to several friends about this and they would say Tavi don't let him get to you. Ladies if a man is constantly tearing you down, but constantly wanting to be with you he has insecurities of his own. He was constantly making me feel like I wasn't pretty, and making me doubt myself yet he wanted to be with me.

I didn't get it how could I allow someone that's not that attractive make me feel unattractive? How could I allow myself to feed into this negative energy? I was taught that you don't have to receive everything someone tell you. I quietly started in my spirit rebuking every negative thing he said.

I remember one time he told me that I was a curse, and he often told me that I had a messed up life. I would be hurt by his comments and

I would cry. Until I realized what God I served, and what he says about me. I'm fearfully and wonderfully made so how can I have a messed up life? I'm made in God's image, so there can be nothing wrong with me.

I have learned that I can't allow what a man says discourage me or make me feel less of who I am. For I am Octavia Denise Hardaway, I'm God's daughter. I will walk into the purpose he has promised me. I realize that everyone has a day, and I know that one day these people that hurt me will have reap what they sow. I will pray for them because God has brought me through these things.

I didn't get strength until I looked deep down inside of me until I learned that if I let people know that they are getting to me, then they are the winner. I guess because beside my Mom and my siblings I really don't have anybody that I can depend on. There have been times I walked long distances because I didn't have one person I know I could call on to pick me up. I was bitter at a time. All I do is help people, and where are they when I needed them? I guess I allowed him to treat me this way because I know he would help me in a situation if I was stuck.

Don't get me wrong God has blessed me with a loving church family, and I'm blessed to have some real friends that have my back. I have learned never accept mistreatment no matter what the situation is you should love yourself more than that! I had to learn that. I am now embracing and loving Octavia more than ever.

There may be a young lady that's reading this book and you made not know what way to turn I declare if you give it all to God you will feel so much better. Stand up for what you believe in and don't waiver and he will bring you through just like he always does. God has brought me through so many test and trials and if he did it for me he will do the same thing for you.

I pray that this book has blessed someone, and I pray that it has encouraged someone as well. I am glad that I took the time to write this to encourage someone. Others things God has brought me through he has brought me through depression. In 2010 my last semester of college started battling with depression and I was worried if I was going to graduate because I had been batting with depression. God extended his mercy and his grace towards me and he anointed my mind and I graduated with a 3.5 Grade Point Average. I earned my Bachelor Science Degree in Political Science, and Criminal Justice. I can testify to someone that God is a keeper and a sustainer! He has anointed me and strengthened me beyond what I could ever imagine. He is working on me and bringing me through this battle of low self-esteem.

Now I would like to offer some encouragement. Ladies stand up and know your worth. Never settle for less than you deserve. Never let a man justify or make you feel you are what he says you are. Know that God made you fearfully and wonderfully made. Embrace the love that Jesus have for you, and learn that there is no pain that he can't heal and bring you through. I'm a living witness. God has brought me through so many things you have seen the pain behind the life of Octavia D.

About the Author:

Octavia Denise Hardaway was born on June 13th 1986 in Akron,

Ohio, to Milton and Margaret Hardaway. Octavia was a 2004 graduate

of John R. Buchtel High school. Octavia immediately went on to

establish her college career at the University of Akron. Hardaway,

graduated May 2010 with Bachelor of Science Degrees in Political

Science and Criminal Justice. Octavia is now a Grad student majoring in

Integrated Language Arts. Octavia received the gift of the Holy Ghost

July 13th 1997, and states this is the turning point of her life. "I was

empty growing up I wasn't complete until the day I received the gift of

the Holy Ghost. In 2010 Octavia started her own ministry in which she

does everything out of her own pocket RHEA. Octavia is a minister, and

an intercessor. Octavia is a member of the New Spirit Revival Center-

Akron Campus. Octavia has a heart that seeks after God. Although she is

very shy and meek she has a great big heart! Octavia's dreams are

reaching the broken and making them feel whole again by her love and

passion for Christ. Octavia understands what it is like to be forgotten and overlooked. "God is a God of second chances, and do overs so I feel like individuals should be givers of second chances and do overs as well". Octavia can reach any crowd whether its children, adults, or the elderly. She has a great big heart, and with the help of God it will allow her to go far. Octavia continue to walk into the favor that God has placed over your life!